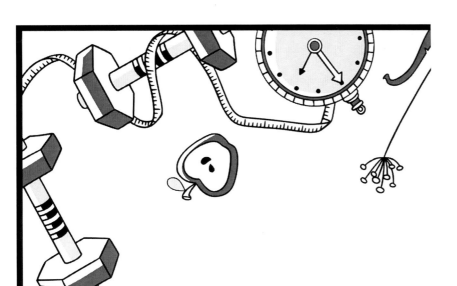

YOGA FOR KIDS

36 Fun Poses To Help Children Exercise, Increase Flexibility, and Practice Mindfulness

CHLOE HANSEN

WiZO
LEARNING

Please consider writing a review!
Just go to: activitywizo.com/review

ISBN: 978-1-951806-90-3

FREE BONUS

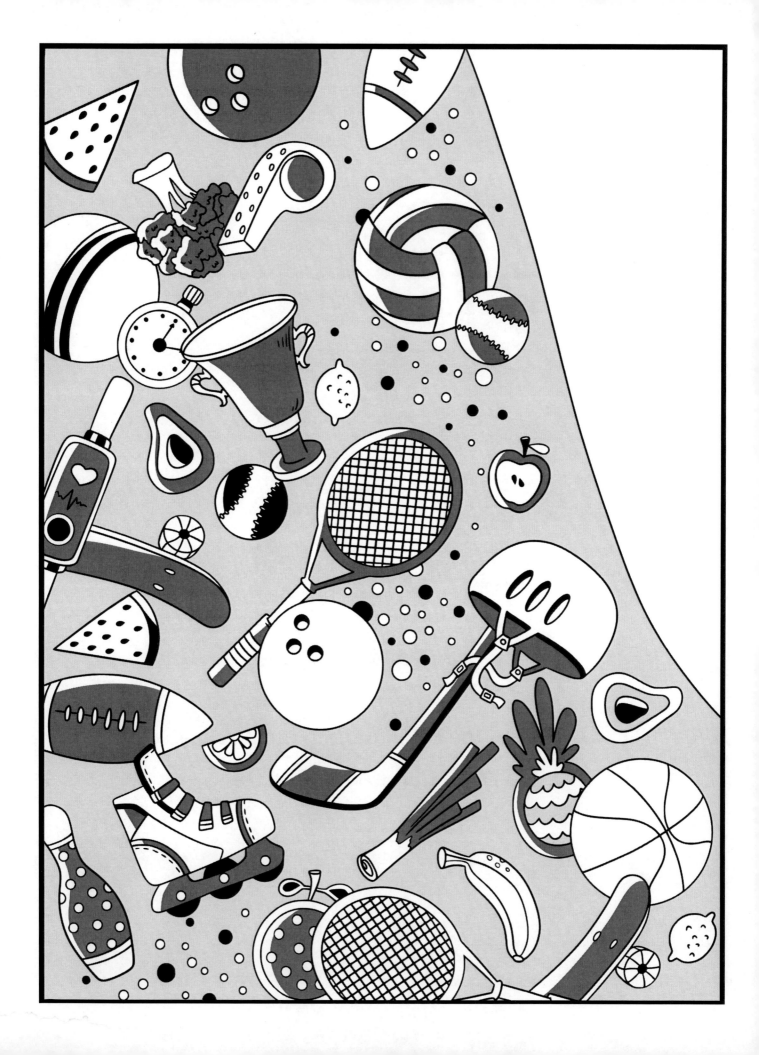

Table of Contents

Introduction

Yoga began as a form of meditation in ancient India. There is written proof of its practice over 5,000 years ago! But it is believed by some, that yoga is closer to a 10,000-year-old practice, as it is mentioned in an ancient text, the Rigveda.

Yoga began as a practice to gain mastery over one's mind, body, and emotions. The word yoga comes from the Sanskrit word "yuj." Yuj means, "to join or yoke." Yogic scriptures say the purpose of yoga is to lead to perfect harmony between the body, mind, and nature.

Between 800 A.D. and 1700 A.D., a style known as hatha yoga came about, and it is hatha yoga that gave birth to modern-day yoga. The style refers to the physical poses a person takes with their body and pairs those poses with breathing techniques.

Between 1700 A.D. and 1900 A.D., hatha yoga became extremely popular. By the 1900s, hatha was adopted by many in the world's Western cultures. Hatha yoga is the style of yoga practiced in most yoga studios. The word "hatha" means willful or forceful and suggests balance, as "ha" stands for the sun and "tha" means moon.

Yoga provides many benefits for those who practice it. It creates a sense of calm and relaxation, helps with balance, and builds physical strength. Yoga can also help people sleep better and have more energy and better concentration.

While yoga is used by many who practice Hinduism, Buddhism, and Jainism, millions of people outside these religions benefit from yoga. It has become a mainstream form of fitness and exercise in Western culture, and people can find classes of all shapes, styles, and sizes.

The typical yoga class lasts anywhere from 45-90 minutes, but you can get started by just doing 10-15 minutes a day a few days a week. Studies have shown that only 12 minutes of yoga a few times a week increases your bone strength and 20 minutes improves your memory and focus.

Whether you seek a way to relieve stress, build your flexibility, increase your energy, or simply have fun, yoga is a form of exercise accessible to all people.

What You Can Expect from This Book

This book is for everyone, not just kids! If you're a teacher looking to add some yoga and physical fitness into your classroom, or a parent who wants to start doing yoga at home with your children, this book is for you, too!

Whoever you are, if you desire to learn yoga, this book will help. The book is broken down into three sections of poses: easy, intermediate, and advanced. Illustrations and step-by-step instructions accompany each pose to guide you in your practice. The fourth chapter contains information about eating healthy for kids, yoga clothing, equipment, and additional resources.

If any of these poses are challenging, modify them in a way that makes your body feel comfortable. If you need to, hold onto a chair or a wall to keep your balance. Use the illustrations as guidance, but don't worry if you don't look exactly like the pictures. There is no wrong way to do yoga unless you are not doing it at all or something is causing you pain.

Yoga should never be painful. If something hurts or you feel a sharp stabbing pain, you should stop. You will, however, feel your muscles stretch and tighten and even burn a little. Your muscles may even feel a little sore the next day; that is normal and okay! Remember to drink lots of water while practicing yoga. You may not always sweat, but your body is working hard.

Yoga can be done by children and adults of all ages, body shapes, heights, and abilities. Use this book to discover the poses that work best for you and make you feel the best!

We hope that as you read through this book and experiment with the poses in these pages, you will develop a love of yoga and create your own unique yoga routines to come back to time and time again.

Yoga for Children

Yes! Yoga for children. Yoga is so beneficial for people of all ages but especially for children. Why? Yoga requires the use of many muscles and gross motor skills children are developing and defining. Yoga helps children work on coordination, balance, flexibility, core strength, and leg, arm, shoulder, hip, and whole-body strength.

Yoga is also incredibly calming, and those calming effects work on kids, too. Children who engage in yoga learn a method to control stress and anxiety, which boosts emotional regulation. Yoga is proven to increase memory and retention skills and boost self-esteem.

A recent 2017 study showed that participating in yoga improved children's executive functions. Executive functions are memory, self-control, ability to handle emotions, and flexibility in thinking. Children who are relaxed and calm will function better in school, and yoga is a great tool to achieve those benefits.

Yoga also promotes mindfulness, which is another excellent way for children to work on focus, emotional regulation, and relaxation. As children participate in yoga, they develop more finely tuned body awareness and a healthy relationship with exercise and physical fitness.

According to the CDC, children ages 6 to 17 should be engaged in a minimum of 60 minutes of physical activity per day with at least three days a week of muscle- and bone-strengthening activities. Preschool children ages 3 to 5 should have physical activity interspersed throughout their day at regular intervals. Participating in a 10-minute yoga routine a few times a week is an excellent way to help meet any child's fitness goals.

More and more schools and early childhood programs have incorporated yoga into their physical and mental health curriculums because the benefits are numerous! You do not need a professional yoga instructor to teach yoga to children.

Yoga is also beneficial for teachers and parents for decreasing stress levels, so while you teach the children in your life some new poses, you will gain muscle strength, coordination, and increased memory as well!

When adults participate in fitness with children, they are the role models for physical fitness and a healthy relationship with exercise and the body. The younger a child learns the importance of physical activity, the more likely it will grow to become a life-long-habit.

Yoga is fun, relaxing, and accessible to all, making it the perfect starter routine for children to delve into fitness!

Chapter 1
Easy

Cat Pose:

Step one: Get down on your hands and knees and spread your fingers wide. Place the top of your feet flat against the floor. Make sure your hands are placed directly under your shoulders. Keep your back as straight (like a tabletop) as you can.

Step two: Arch your back up towards the ceiling like a cat stretching its back. As you round your back, tuck your head down and look at your tummy. Pull your tummy in as you arch your back up. Remember to keep breathing! Hold it for a few seconds, then relax. Repeat the stretch a few more times.

Cat pose is an excellent stretch for your back and helps build your tummy muscles! It is a great stretch to use in the morning to help you wake up. If you have a cat at home, watch them the next time they stretch, and you'll see just how much like a cat you look while performing this pose!

Cat Pose

Chair Pose

Step one: Stand up nice and tall with your legs close together but not touching and your arms relaxed at your sides. As you stand tall, imagine a string coming out of the top of your head, pulling your head and your spine straight. Keep your head facing forward.

Step two: Slowly bend your knees as if you were going to sit in an imaginary chair. As you "sit," try to keep your back, neck, and head as straight as possible.

Step three: Once you are holding the seated position, slowly raise your arms towards the sky. Hold the stretch for a few seconds, then relax. Repeat it a few more times.

This one can make it tricky to maintain your balance, but it is a great exercise to strengthen your toes and feet! It may take some practice to get the chair pose, but keep trying, and you will master it.

Chair Pose

Child's Pose

Step one: Sit down on the floor with your knees tucked under your body. Your bottom should be resting upon your heels. Sit up nice and tall with your head looking forward and keep your spine straight.

Step two: Calmly reach your arms straight up towards the ceiling. As you reach your arms up, feel your spine stretch and elongate.

Step three: Slowly bend your torso forward, keeping your arms straight as you lean down. Stretch your arms out in front of you, and let your nose touch the ground. Hold the stretch, keeping your fingers close together. Take some deep breaths in through your nose and out through your mouth as you stretch.

Child's pose is a calming and relaxing pose and a great one to use if you feel angry or stressed. It can also be a great stretch to do in the morning to warm your body up for the day.

Childs Pose

Cobra Pose

Step one: Lie face-down on the floor or your yoga mat, and let your nose gently touch the ground. Your arms should be lying loosely at your sides, and the tops of your feet should be gently pressing into the floor.

Step two: Like a snake, slide or slither your hands forward until they are next to your shoulders. Take a deep breath in through your nose and blow slowly out your mouth.

Step three: Take another deep breath in through your nose, and as you do, use your arms to push your chest up off the floor. Push your arms down into the floor as you push your chest up and pull your neck back to look like a giant king cobra! After holding the pose a few moments, lie back down on the floor, and repeat a few times.

Cobra pose feels very good in your back and chest and stretches your arms out, too!

Cobra Pose

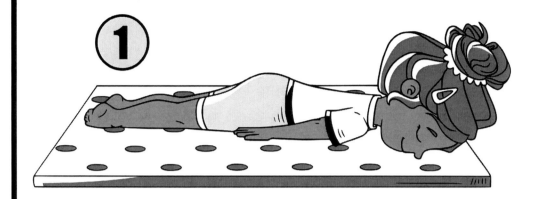

Cow Pose

Step one: Get down on all fours with your hands and knees on the ground. Keep your hands in a direct line under your shoulders. Press the tops of your feet gently into the floor, and keep your back flat, just like you did with the cat pose and your head looking straight in front of you.

Step two: Push your tummy towards the floor as your arch your neck and head upwards. Your bottom should be slightly higher than your back. Hold the pose for a few moments, then return your back and head to the straightened position.

This pose can be tricky to do at first, so looking in a mirror might help you get the right posture.

Cow pose is very similar to cat pose, and the two are often done together, going back and forth between them to create an excellent stretch for your back!

Cow Pose

Downward Facing Dog

Step one: This pose begins in a similar position to the cat and cow poses. Get down on all fours with your hands placed directly under your shoulders. Remember to breathe in through your nose and out through your mouth.

Step two: At the same time, slide your hands slightly forward and push your bottom in the air, keeping your knees over your ankles. Press your hands into the floor and relax your head and neck. You should be able to see your toes! After holding the stretch for a few seconds, come back down on all fours and repeat.

Downward facing dog is one of the most popular yoga poses, and it can help you calm down when feeling angry or stressed. Any time you create inversion in your body, putting your head below your waist, the position increases blood and oxygen to your brain. The extra blood and oxygen boost your brainpower!

Downward Facing Dog

Easy Pose

Step one: Sit down on your yoga mat or the floor and stretch your legs out in front of you like a V. Your legs shouldn't be stretched too wide; it should be a relaxed and comfortable position. Try to keep your back and neck straight; imagine an invisible string pulling you up through the top of your head.

Step two: Slide your legs towards you and sit up straight with your legs crisscrossed. Rest your hands comfortably on top of your knees and relax. Close your eyes and take some deep breaths in through your nose and out through your mouth. Hold this pose as long as it feels comfortable.

Easy pose is just that; it's easy! It is a great pose to put in the middle of your routine as a break. Many people also use this pose to begin and end their yoga routine. It is also a comfortable pose to hold while you just think through your thoughts.

Extended Mountain Pose

Step one: Stand up nice and tall on your yoga mat with your legs under your shoulders. You need a solid base in your legs to become a strong mountain. Remember to take deep breaths in through your nose and out through your mouth.

Step two: Reach your arms forward, and gently bring them up to reach towards the sky. Your arms should be right next to your ears. Stretch your arms as high as they will go, but keep your feet firmly planted to the floor. As you reach up, face the palms of your hands upwards. Bend your chest and tummy slightly backward like you are taking in the sunshine. Hold the stretch for a few seconds, then relax your arms down and start again.

Mountain pose is sometimes called giraffe, sun salutation, or fountain pose. Imagine yourself any one of those things as you hold this incredible-feeling stretch.

Extended Mountain Pose

Happy Baby Pose

Step one: Lie down on your back on top of your yoga mat or the floor. Let your arms rest gently at your sides and look straight up at the ceiling. Make yourself feel like one long line. Take a moment and inhale a few deep breaths in through your nose and out through your mouth. Enjoy the stillness of just being there.

Step two: Using your core or tummy muscles, pull your legs towards you, so your knees are over your chest. Your legs should be bent and slightly relaxed.

Step three: Bring your arms up from the sides and grab the bottoms of your feet, pull gently on your feet, bringing your knees towards your armpits. Keep your back pressed flat against the floor and enjoy some deep breaths while you feel this tremendous massaging stretch.

Happy baby pose is a very calming pose and gives your hips a nice stretch.

Happy Baby Pose

Hero Pose

Step one: Sit down on your yoga mat or the floor with your knees on either side of you. If that is uncomfortable, place your legs under you, and sit on your knees with your bottom resting on your heels. Gently rest your hands on your knees. Take a few deep breaths in through your nose and out through your mouth.

Step two: Reach your arms out in front of you, lace your fingers together, and twist your hands inside out. Push your hands outward like a superhero shooting their strength forward. Feel the stretch in your arms as you push outwards.

Step three: Keeping your fingers laced together, slowly raise your arms above your head. Keep your head facing forward. Close your eyes as you take deep breaths and feel your superhero muscles growing stronger. After holding the stretch for a few seconds, slowly rotate your upper body from side to side.

Hero pose is an excellent way to stretch your arms and your shoulders.

Hero Pose

33

Horse Stance

Step one: Kneel on your yoga mat or the floor with one leg bent in front of you and one leg on the floor. Press only the toes of your back foot into the floor, and firmly place your whole front foot on the mat. Keep your back and spine long and straight. You should be looking straight ahead.

Step two: Slowly raise your arms in front of you into a prayer position. Take a moment to take a few deep breaths in through your nose and out through your mouth.

Step three: Reach your arms out to the sides, and slowly raise them until your hands touch in the prayer pose above your head. Gently press your fingertips together as you hold the pose. When you are ready, slowly lower your arms down to your sides, switch legs, and repeat.

Horse pose is an excellent way to work on your balance and get an incredible arm stretch at the same time!

Horse Stance

Kneeling

Step one: Kneel on the mat with your knees on either side of you and your hands gently resting on top of your legs. If this is uncomfortable, place your knees directly beneath you and let your bottom rest on your heels.

Step two: Slowly raise your arms towards the sky, reaching as high as you can as you stretch out your back and straighten your spine. Your arms should be directly next to your ears. You can repeat the arm raises a few times, gently bringing them down and then back up. Each time you raise your arms to the top, take a deep breath in through the nose. Hold your breath and the pose for two to three seconds, and then breathe out through your mouth as you lower them.

Kneeling is another wonderful way to begin or end your yoga session or if you just need a few moments to center your thoughts and stretch.

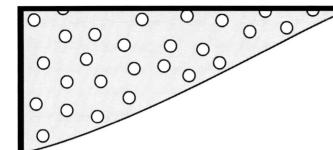

Chapter 2

Intermediate

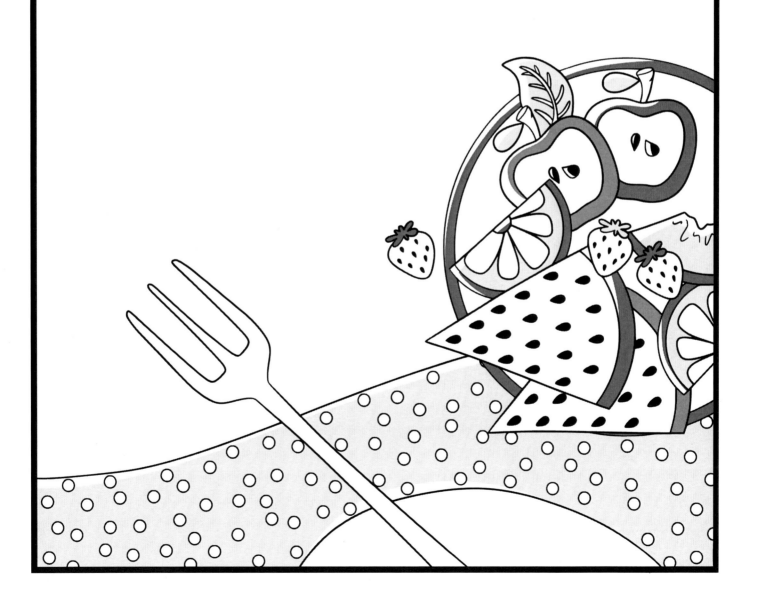

Bridge Pose

Step one: Lie flat on your back on your yoga mat or the floor and look up at the ceiling. Take a few deep breaths in through your nose and out through your mouth as you relax your body. Your legs should be straight out in front of you, and your arms should be resting gently at your side.

Step two: Move both your legs into a bent position and slightly lift your bottom up but not entirely off of the floor. Make sure you tighten the muscles in your stomach and continue to breathe.

Step three: Press your arms firmly into the floor as you raise your bottom and back entirely off of the floor. Hold this pose for a count of five, then return your bottom to the floor, leaving your legs bent. Practice a few times by lifting your bottom and back, holding, and returning it to the floor.

If this pose is challenging, at first lift your back only as far as it is comfortable. The more you practice, the easier it will become.

Bridge Pose

1

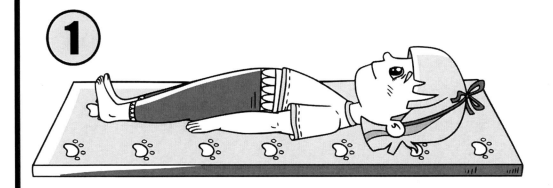

2

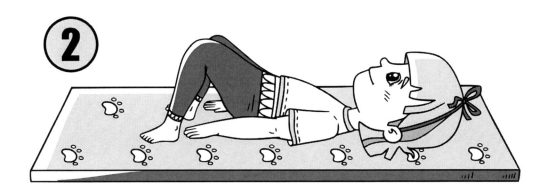

3

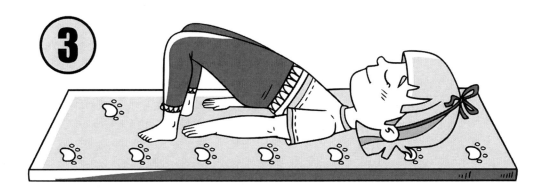

Knees to Chest

Step one: Lie flat on your back on top of your yoga mat or the floor. Look straight up at the ceiling as you keep your legs and arms relaxed. Take a few deep breaths in through your nose and out through your mouth.

Step two: Once you feel relaxed, pull your knees towards your chest. Wrap your arms around your knees and hug them to your chest. You can hold this pose still or rock side to side slightly if that feels comfortable.

This stretch is beneficial for your back and your hamstrings — the upper section of your leg. You can also do this stretch by only pulling back one leg at a time. When you leave one leg on the floor, it provides an anchor and better balance for your body, so if you feel a little wobbly, try just stretching one leg at a time.

Knees To Chest

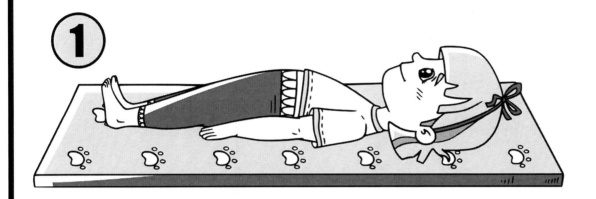

Dolphin Pose

Step one: Get down on your hands and knees on the floor. Align your shoulders over your hands and your bottom over your knees. Your legs should be close together but not touching one another. Keep your back as flat as a table and hold for a few seconds.

Step two: Bend the front half of your body down towards the floor. As you bend forward, keep your shoulders above your hands and keep your back in a straight line. If you look in the mirror, your bottom to your head should look like a diagonal line.

Step three: Continue bending forward until your head touches the mat and your legs are fully extended. Your bottom should be way up in the air, with the top of your head touching the mat. As you extend your bottom, keep your forearms flat against the mat.

As you complete this pose, imagine yourself a dolphin cresting out of the water. If you've never seen a dolphin jump in and out of the ocean, find a picture or video to watch!

Dolphin Pose

Downhill Skier

Step one: Stand up tall on your yoga mat with your feet shoulder-width apart. Your arms should be hanging loosely at your sides. Keep your neck elongated and your head looking straight forward. Imagine you are about to ski down a big, fast hill!

Step two: Bend your knees slightly and bend your torso forward. At the same time, bring your arms forward, keeping your elbows close to your body. You can sway side-to-side a little as if you were skiing down a hill. Adding the additional movement will strengthen your balance and core muscles. When ready, stand up straight and try the pose again.

An alternate way to do this position is to hold your arms straight back behind you. Holding your arms behind you will provide you with a nice stretch in your elongated arms. You can alternate between both arm positions each time you create the pose.

Downhill Skier

Eagle Pose

Step one: Start by standing on your yoga mat and finding your center and balancing. Reach your arms out wide to the side like an eagle spreading its wings, and cross one leg over the other. Choose whichever leg is easier for you to cross without wobbling too much.

Step two: Take a moment to make sure you have your balance and enjoy a few deep breaths in through your nose and out through your mouth. Then, bring your arms together and cross them over one another in front of your chest.

Step three: Slowly bend down on your anchor leg while leaning forward slightly. Close your eyes and enjoy the stretch all over! Return to a standing position and switch your leg and arm positions and try again.

This pose can be tricky, especially if you struggle with your balance. If crossing your legs is difficult, try doing the pose with both legs on the floor. You can also leave your arms out wide as you practice folding one leg over the other and bending down. Both modifications will help you with your balance.

Eagle Pose

Extended Child's Pose

Step one: Sit down on the floor with your knees on either side of your body. Your bottom should be resting between your heels. This is different from the original child's pose, where your bottom rests on your heels. Sit up nice and tall with your head looking forward and keep a straight spine.

Step two: Calmly reach your arms straight up towards the ceiling. As you reach your arms up, feel your spine stretch and elongate.

Step three: This another differentiation from the original child's pose. Instead of merely leaning forward and touching your forehead to the ground, you are going to elongate your torso (chest and belly) and lie them flat on the mat as well. Reach your arms out straight ahead, keeping them next to your ears.

If it is more comfortable to keep your bottom on your heels, then adjust the pose accordingly, however, if you are able to put your knees on either side of you, it will provide a different stretch and one that is excellent for your hips!

Extended Child's Pose

51

Extended Cat Pose

Step one: Get down on your hands and knees on your yoga mat or the floor. Your bottom should be directly over your knees, with your legs slightly apart. Place your shoulders in a straight line over your hands and extend your neck to look straight ahead. Take time to center your balance before moving on to step two.

Step two: Keeping everything aligned and your head still looking straight out in front, slowly raise one of your legs and extend it straight behind you. Keep the leg that makes you feel the most stable on the ground first.

Step three: When you feel ready, slowly extend the arm opposite of the leg you have extended; if you have your right leg extended, you will also extend your left arm. Hold the pose for a count of five if you can, then return both your arm and leg to the floor. Repeat the pose by extending your other leg and arm.

It will likely be easier for one side of your body than the other to maintain balance; that is very normal. Take your time and try again. If it helps, practice just extending your legs first until you feel confident with your balance, then add the arms into the pose. Every stretch is a good stretch and will make your body stronger, so don't worry about making each pose perfect!

Extended Cat Pose

1

2

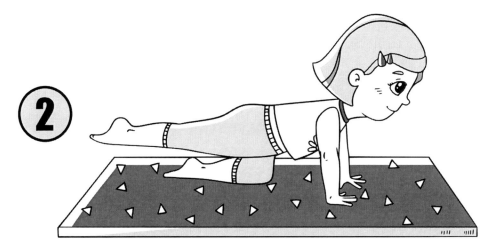

3

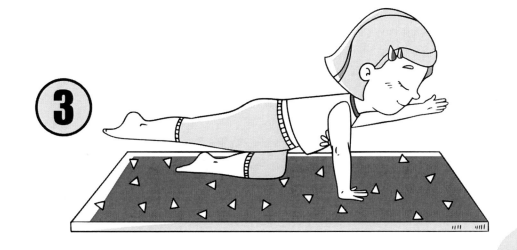

Gyan Mudra

Step one: Sit comfortably on your yoga mat with your legs out in front of you in V shape. Your hands should be resting gently on your lap. Keep a long straight neck as you look forward.

Step two: Slide your legs toward you into a comfortable crisscross pattern and rest the backs of your wrists upon your knees. Touch your index fingertips (finger closest to the thumb) and your thumb gently together. Keep your other three fingers slightly stretched but still relaxed. Close your eyes, and you take several deep breaths in through your nose and out through your mouth.

Mudras are specific hand positions used in yoga to direct specific energy into your body. "Gyan" means knowledge. Use this pose when you want to focus your mind during your yoga or meditation practice. This pose is a common one used by individuals as they sit and meditate.

Gyan Mudra

Lotus Pose

Step one: Sit on the floor or your yoga mat and pull one of your legs towards you. Pull your heel up so that it is resting in our lap. Keep your neck in a long line and look straight ahead.

Step two: Pull your other leg towards you and pull it over the top of the leg already in your lap. Position the second heel so it is resting on your thighs. Getting both legs into this position can be difficult for some, and some people can only do it with a specific leg on top and bottom. Try switching your legs around to see what is most comfortable for you.

Step three: Place your hands gently on your knees and touch the tips of your index fingers to the tips of your thumbs. Spread out the other three fingers, keeping them slightly relaxed. This hand position is the gyan mudras from the pose above. Close your eyes and take deep breaths in through your nose and out through your mouth. Take your time and settle into this position and relax.

If this position is difficult for you, try just pulling in one leg at a time until it becomes comfortable for you to rest it on your thigh.

Lotus Pose

Seated Forward Bend

Step one: Sit down on your yoga mat or the floor with your legs straight out in front of you. You should flex your toes towards the ceiling, and your head should be looking straight ahead. Picture your back as a long line as you keep your spine straight and tall.

Step two: As you take a deep breath in through your nose, raise your arms up towards the sky. Your elbow should be next to your ears but not touching. Elongate and extend your fingers upwards, giving your hands a nice stretch.

Step three: As you breathe out through your mouth, bend your body forward. Keep your arms straight as you bend and try to touch your nose to your knees. If you cannot bend down that far, that's ok; bend as far as you can comfortably. You should feel a stretch but never pain. If you can, reach your hands out and gently wrap them around the bottoms of your feet. When you are ready, take a deep breath in and sit up to start the pose over again.

This pose is an excellent all-over body stretch. During different steps, you will feel it in your arms, back, hands, and legs!

Seated Forward Bend

1

2

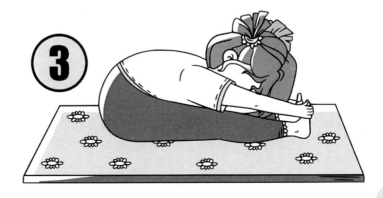

3

Standing Forward Bend

Step one: Stand up nice and tall on your yoga mat and reach your arms up high. Keep your arms slightly angled so that your elbows are beside your cheeks. Your legs should be close together, touching, if possible.

Step two: Take a deep breath in through your nose and as you exhale out of your mouth, bend forward, and reach your hands towards the ground. If possible, wrap your fingers under the bottoms of your feet. Only bend as far forward as is comfortable. When you are ready, take a deep breath in through your nose and return to the starting position.

Remember, yoga should never cause you pain. If you feel any pain, you should stop your bend and back up a little because it means you have reached your flexibility point. The more you practice yoga, the more flexible you will become, so don't give up!

Standing Forward Bend

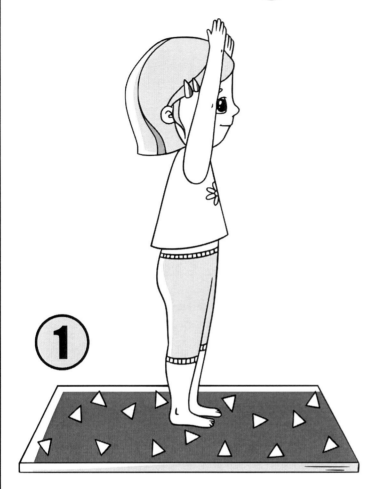

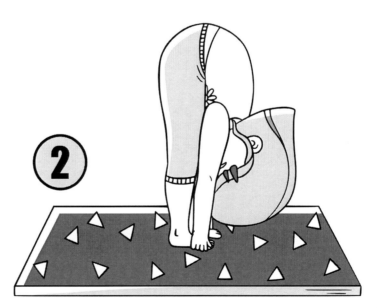

Squat Pose

Step one: Stand up nice and tall with your feet a little bit apart and your head facing forward. The top of your head all the way down your spine should feel like one long, straight line. Press your palms together in front of your heart and take a few deep breaths in through your nose and out through your mouth. You can close your eyes if that feels good!

Step two: When you are ready, slowly lower your body to the ground and squat, keeping your bottom off the ground. Your arms should remain in front of you with your palms still pressed together in front of your heart. If you find it difficult to squat with your arms in the position, put them out to your sides as you get into the squat position, and then return them to the place in front of your heart.

Picture yourself like a little frog or toad about to dive into a cool pond as you hold this position.

Squat Pose

Chapter 3

Advanced

Boat Pose

Step one: Sit down on your yoga mat or the floor with your knees bent and your legs out in front of you. Lean gently back on your arms with your elbows slightly bent. Your fingers should be facing your bottom.

Step two: Using your arms for support, engage your core muscles (your tummy muscles) and slowly raise your legs off of the floor. Keep your knees bent and point your toes away from you.

Step three: If you feel stable, lift your arms off the ground and reach them out in front of you. Gently rest the palms of your hands against the outside of your knees. Hold this pose for several seconds if you can, and imagine you are a boat floating on a lake or in the ocean.

This pose requires a lot of engagement from your abdominal or core muscles. Our core muscles help with our posture, and they help support our back.

Boat Pose

Bow Pose

Step one: Lie face down on your yoga mat with your forehead and nose touching the mat and your arms lying loosely at your sides. Your legs should be close together and in a flat line.

Step two: At the same time, bend your legs towards you with your heels right over your bottom and reach back and grab your feet. Hold this stretch for a moment or two before moving on.

Step three: When you are ready, pull your legs towards you even further as you arch your back and bring your chest off the mat. Keep your shoulders down away from your ears while drawing your shoulder blades towards each other.

Bow pose is an excellent all-over pose, as it stretches everything from your ankles to your thighs, chest, neck, and back. This is a great stretch to help improve your posture.

Bow Pose

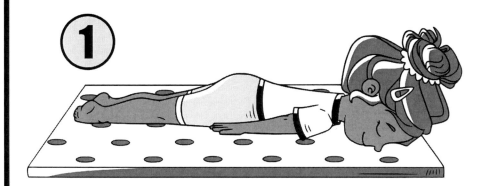

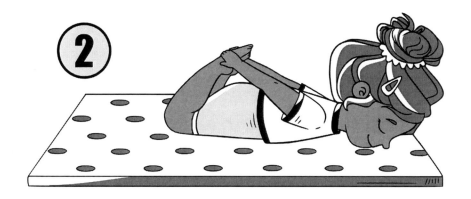

Crescent Moon Pose

Step one: Stand up on your yoga mat with your feet shoulder-width apart and firmly planted on the ground. Let your arms rest gently at your sides and elongate your neck with your head looking straight ahead. Enjoy the posture of standing straight and tall for a few moments.

Step two: Bend your torso (middle section of your body) slightly to the side as you bring your hands over your head. Push your hips in the opposite direction of your arms and press your palms together as you stretch your arms in the same direction your body is leaning. Hold the pose for a few seconds, then return to the starting position before repeating it on the other side of your body.

The crescent moon pose elongates your side and really gives your arms and torso an excellent stretch. This is a great one to help you wake up or stretch out your body if you've been sitting too long!

Crescent Moon Pose

Dancer's Pose

Step one: Begin by standing up straight and tall on your mat with your feet close together. Allow one arm to rest gently at your side as you reach the other arm up towards the sky. Your arm that is reaching up should be at a slight angle forward, not completely vertical.

Step two: Reach behind you with the arm that is down and bend the same leg up and grasp your foot with your hand. Keep your heel away from your bottom; your arm and leg should be making a hole.

Step three: Once you feel stable and solid with your balance, lean your body forward slightly, reaching your back leg a little higher into the air. When you are ready, return your foot to the floor and repeat the pose on the other side of your body.

This one can be tricky if you struggle with your balance; remember to take your time and do what feels comfortable. If you need help with this one, use the arm that is reaching into the air to hold onto the wall or a shelf.

Dancer's Pose

Dancing Ganesha

Step one: Plant your feet firmly on your yoga mat about shoulder's width apart and rest your arms down at your sides. Feel your back nice and tall in a straight line and keep your head looking forward. Take a moment to make sure your stance is strong.

Step two: Bring your hands together so that your wrists are touching one on top of the other and front to back; one hand should be pointing up, and the other should be pointing down.

Step three: Slowly lift the leg on the same side as the hand facing up and cross it in front of your other knee. Twist your ankle so your foot is pointing away from your body. Hold this pose for a few moments, then return to the starting position, and repeat on the other side.

Dancing Ganesha requires balance, and it may be challenging to get the pose right at first. You can use a mirror to help you see your body and the shapes it is making. This pose is named after the Hindu god of the same name, portrayed as a dancing elephant. Ganesha promotes self-esteem, confidence, and inner strength. Think of all those powerful attributes when you do this pose!

Dancing Ganesha

Extended Side Angle Pose

Step one: Stand on your yoga mat with one leg extended behind you in a straight line and the other bent in front of you. The bent leg's knee should be directly over your toes so that if you drew a line from toe to knee, it would be straight. Rest your arms at your side and look straight ahead.

Step two: Lean into the bended knee slightly and raise your arms. The arm of the bent knee should be out front and the other arm stretched behind you.

Step three: With the arm in front of you, bend down and press your palm into the floor. Your arm should be in front of your knee with your palm next to your heel. Your other arm should be reaching straight up towards the ceiling. Turn your head up and look up towards the hand stretched high. When ready, return to standing and switch sides to repeat.

The extended side angle pose is another one that stretches the whole body. Whole-body stretches are an excellent way to engage several muscles at once and to energize your body and mind.

Extended Side Angle Pose

Flower Pose

Step one: Sit down on your yoga mat or the floor with your knees bent in front of you. Place your arms behind you and lean back slightly. Place your fingers away from your bottom.

Step two: Lift your legs up and reach your arms underneath to support your legs. Keep your back straight and try to maintain your balance on your bottom. Try to hold this pose for several seconds (longer if you can), then return your feet and arms to the floor before trying again.

Flower pose is challenging primarily because it requires so much core (tummy strength) and balance. Do the best you can, and take your time learning this pose. If you are having difficulty keeping both your arms and legs off the floor, try simply raising your legs first and holding them in the upright position. The more you build up your muscles, the easier this pose will become.

Flower Pose

Half Shoulder Stand

Step one: Lie down on your back and look up at the ceiling. Rest your legs straight out in front of you and rest your arms at your side. Take a few deep breaths in through your nose and out through your mouth.

Step two: Lift your knees up and bend them towards your chest. Keep your toes pointed.

Step three: Slowly lift your legs straight up into the air and try to support your weight on your shoulders. Use your hands to help support your back.

Don't worry if you cannot do this pose initially; simply lift your legs as high in the air as you can. One way you can practice this is to use a wall to help support your legs.

Half Shoulder Stand

Locust Pose

Step one: Lie face down on your yoga mat or a carpeted floor with your nose and forehead resting gently on the floor. Press the tops of your feet into the floor and rest your arms gently at your side. Take your time and enjoy a few deep breaths in through your nose and out through your mouth.

Step two: When you're ready, arch your chest and legs off the floor, and reach your arms back behind you. Keep your legs close together as your arch them up. Hold this stretch for a few moments and return your body to the floor. When you're ready, try the pose again.

As you do this stretch, really feel it in your chest. Imagine you're flying like a bug or a superhero as you hold this pose.

Locust Pose

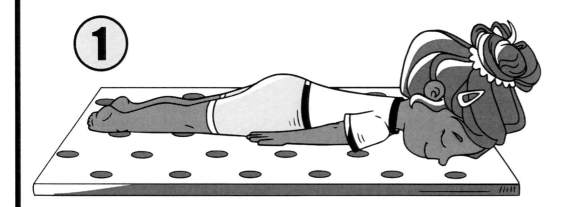

Lunge Pose

Step one: Stand up straight and tall on your yoga mat or the floor. Extend one leg in front of you and bend your knee. Your knee should be directly over your toes. Allow your arms to rest at your sides.

Step two: Slowly raise your arms up in the air, keeping them straight. They should be angled slightly forward with your elbows next to your cheeks.

Step three: Lean forward, bring your arms down to the ground, and press your palms to the floor. Try to keep a long straight line from the back of your heel all the way up to the top of your head. When you are ready, return to the starting position and switch legs.

This is an excellent stretch for your back and legs. As you do this pose, imagine you are a runner about to start a race.

Lunge Pose

Pigeon Pose

Step one: Sit on the floor with your legs crossed. Rest your hands gently on your knees or in your lap.

Step two: Extend one of your legs out in front of you and extend the toes of that foot. Enjoy that long stretch in your leg. Remember to keep your back tall and straight.

Step three: Take that same leg and slide it behind you, so it is stretched out straight. Place your hands down on the floor and lift your chest and push it out. Lift and stretch your neck and look slightly upwards. Enjoy a few deep breaths in through your nose and out through your mouth, then go back to the start position and switch legs.

As you perform this stretch, up open your chest up and lift your heart. Pigeon pose is a very relaxing and calming stretch.

Pigeon Pose

Reverse Table-Top

Step one: Sit on your bottom with your legs bent in front of you and your arms behind you. Your fingers should be facing your bottom. Lean back slightly on your arms for support.

Step two: Lift your bottom off the floor and create a flat table shape with your chest and tummy. Keep your neck supported and look up towards the sky. Hold the position as long as it feels comfortable. Come back down to the floor in the starting position, and when you're ready, try the pose again.

As you perform the reverse table-top, try not to push your belly upwards. Keep the line as straight as possible as you feel the stretch through all of your body.

Reverse Table Top Pose

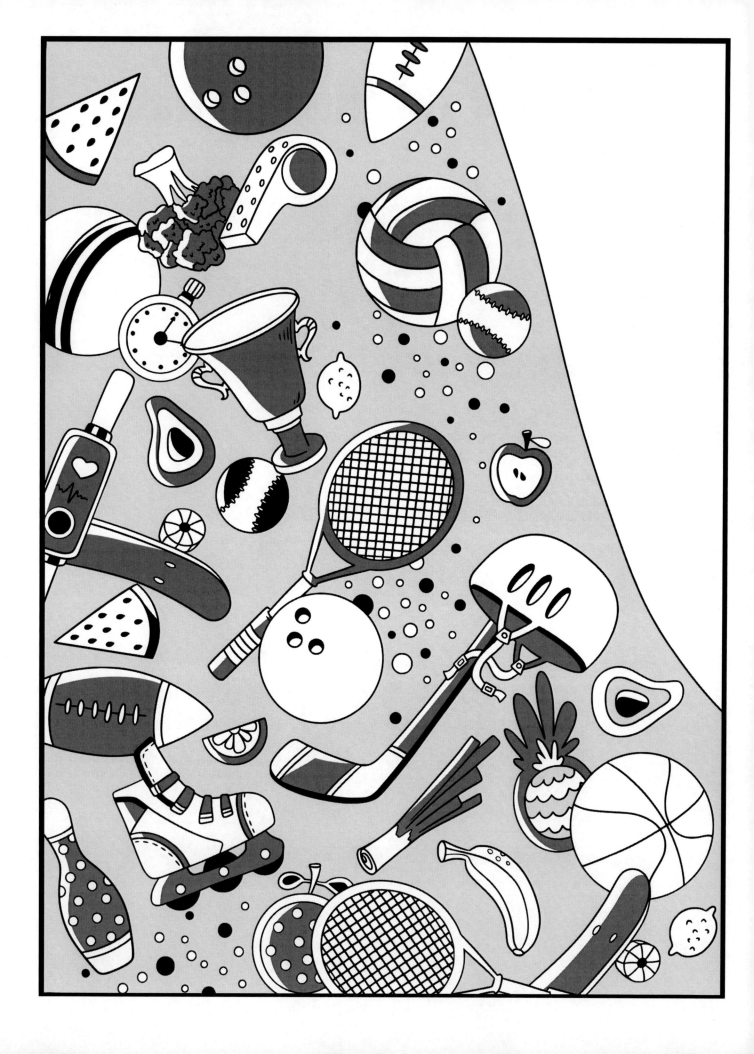

Chapter 4

Healthy Lifestyle

Healthy Lifestyle

If you have read this far, you are ready to make yoga a part of your daily life and ready to engage in a healthy lifestyle. Exercise and fitness are only a piece of the puzzle, but there are many other things we need to do regularly to keep our bodies and minds healthy and strong.

Fitness

Since this book is primarily about yoga, let's start with the fitness aspect of a healthy lifestyle. Physical activity should be part of your daily schedule as a kid. While computers, iPads, TVs, and video games are tempting and can certainly be enjoyed from time to time, young brains and bodies require exercise to reach their full potential.

The Center for Disease Control, or CDC, is the health protection agency of the United States — basically the leading authority on health and wellbeing. The CDC recommends children ages 6 to 16 get at least one hour or 60 minutes a day of physical activity.

This activity should be broken down into three groups:

Cardio or aerobic activity like running, walking, dancing. The goal is to get your heartbeat pumping

Muscle-strengthening — this is where yoga can help, as well as climbing, push-ups, pull-ups, etc.

Bone-strengthening — yoga can also help here! Running and jumping build bone strength, too.

Creating a mix of all three throughout your week is the best way to keep your body fit and healthy!

Other Fitness Ideas:

- Jump-rope (alone or with friends)
- Gymnastics
- Playing on a sports team
- Swimming
- Playing tag
- Riding a bike
- Hiking
- Kayaking
- Martial arts

Healthy Eating

The other key factor in developing a healthy body is proper nutrition. If you are a kid or teen reading this, I am sure your parents have been telling you to eat vegetables your entire life, and guess what? Your parents are right!

Eating healthy doesn't mean you have to get rid of all the junk food and sugar, but much like the use of your electronics, these treats should be limited and enjoyed for fun, not as the main part of your diet.

Fruits and Veggies

Find some fruit and vegetables that you DO like, and make sure mom and dad keep those stocked in the house. While some fruits and veggies are better for you than others, most likely, if they have a color, they are providing you some essential nutrients. Starchy vegetables like corn, potatoes, sweet potatoes, peas, and beans are good for you but should be eaten less frequently than foods like berries, apples, cucumbers, broccoli, carrots, etc.

Protein

Another food that should be a daily part of your diet is lean protein, like chicken breast, turkey, fish, shrimp, eggs, and tofu. Dairy is also a great source of protein but watch out for those sugary flavors because they add a lot of unwanted sugar to your body. You can sweeten up your yogurt with some fruit and little honey, which is a natural sweetener. Dairy should not be counted as part of your lean proteins, instead it is its own category.

Whole Grains

Whole grains are the third part of your healthy eating plan. This means avoiding things like white bread and choosing whole wheat bread instead! Other whole grains you might already eat or would like to try are brown rice, quinoa, popcorn, and some types of oatmeal. You can also purchase whole grain pasta.

A Healthy Plate

Myplate.gov is an excellent resource for information about making a healthy plate. The general guidelines for healthy eating are that half of your plate should be fruits and vegetables, a quarter grains, a quarter lean protein, and two to three cups of dairy a day. A child ages 2 to 8 should have 2-2 ½ cups and children ages 9 to 18 three cups.

The dairy you eat should contain calcium and vitamin D, two essential nutrients to grow and maintain strong bones.

Hydration

Hydration plays a major role in maintaining a healthy body. Hydration means keeping your body full of fluids, but we don't mean sugary juices and sodas. Water is what you should be drinking! Many people say adults should consume eight 8-ounce glasses a day; children ages 9 and up should follow this rule, too!

Younger children can have a little less; if you are between the ages of 4 and 8, you should be drinking five cups a day.

One way to achieve this is to have your parents buy you a fun water bottle that you can carry with you wherever you go. Keeping your water close by will encourage you to drink it!

A Healthy Mind

Maintaining a healthy body also includes maintaining a healthy mind. Exercise and eating right go a long way to help our minds focus and stay sharp, but sometimes we need a little more.

Finding time to relax and engage in activities we enjoy is also very important. When you're busy with homework, extracurricular activities, and chores around the house, stress can begin to creep in. It is important to have some relaxing activities that you enjoy doing. If you don't have time to slow down at the moment, taking some deep breaths can reset your brain and calm your nerves.

Relaxing activities may include reading, making or listening to music, coloring, drawing or painting, gardening, writing, or just sitting with your eyes closed and relaxing.

Mindfulness and mediation are some other things you can do to help strengthen your mind. Talk to your parents about finding mediation specifically for kids for you to listen to and enjoy.

Clothing and Equipment

A yoga mat can make doing yoga much more comfortable, but it is not necessary. If you do not have a yoga mat, you can use an area or throw rug or practice in a room with a carpeted floor. Not only does the mat or carpet provide a cushioning for poses on your knees and back, but it provides a soft place to land should you lose your balance and fall.

There is another type of equipment called yoga blocks people use to help them with some of their poses. Blocks are especially helpful for those who have flexibility issues. As a kid practicing yoga, you probably don't need to buy blocks, but if you think they may be helpful to you, check out athletic supply stores to see what's available.

Wearing comfortable clothing is also a must with yoga. You will be performing a lot of stretches and bends, and you do not want stiff or uncomfortable clothing to get in the way. Leggings, shorts, sweatpants, and athletic pants are all excellent options for your bottom half. On top, a tank top or a t-shirt is all you need!

Many people perform yoga in their bare feet, so don't feel the need to purchase fancy new shoes. Bare feet are usually better than socks because socks can be slippery. Your bare feet are much better at gripping the mat or the floor.

Wrap-up

However you choose to practice yoga, we hope you will enjoy practicing the poses in this book and developing a healthy body and mind!

Yoga can be done anywhere: on the beach, at the park, in your school gym, or your bedroom. Whenever you feel the need to let some stress out and get a good stretch, remember yoga is always there for you, no matter where you are!

Made in United States
North Haven, CT
08 November 2021